Reflections of a Woman's Life

Gypsie-Ami Offenbacher-Ferris

Advance Reviews

"Let us commiserate together in the hope that we will come out the other side happy and whole, or at least intact!"

With this vow, I flip through the pages of this chapbook, *Reflections of a Woman's Life* by Gypsie-Ami Offenbacher-Ferris. It is a deeply intimate and emotionally unflinching chapbook that traces the arc of womanhood, from birth to ageing, from love's first promise to its devastating betrayals, and from motherhood to the painful grace of letting go. As the author clarifies, this is not a "feel-good" book; rather, it is a work of emotional catharsis, written in lived experience.

The opening poem, "The Arrival", is a visceral reimagining of birth, narrated from the infant's sensory perspective. Earth, loam, darkness, and sound function as primal symbols, making birth a miraculous bliss.

"Finally, swaddled protectively held
        in gentle swaying arms,

a presence known but unknown, presses wet."

These lines remind me of the birth of
        my baby boy.

"Chance Encounter" turns on irony and self-recognition. The mirror becomes a symbol of fractured identity and societal expectations placed on women's bodies over time.

"My Garden" takes us to a world where life and death work simultaneously. Beside a blooming flower, a dragonfly lay dead. "Free" is one of the darkest poems in the collection. "Free" confronts illness, addiction, and suicidal ideation, but putting aside these dark themes, there is hope. In "Nibble at the Beach", a romantic moment collapses with the revelation of infidelity. The ocean breeze and golden sunset stand in cruel contrast to betrayal, shattering love in an instant. "A Mother's Nose Noes" celebrates maternal intuition and unconditional love. "Feelings in Colour" celebrates colour: neutral beige, sea-blue eyes, comforting yellow, green bushes, pastel orange, and more. The poem masterfully blends sensory imagery with psychological depth.

Offenbacher-Ferris writes in free verse, favouring clarity over ornamentation. Her strength lies in emotional precision rather than abstraction. Symbols such as gardens, colour, mirrors, light, and darkness are grounded in lived experience. *Reflections of a Woman's Life* is highly recommended for readers who appreciate confessional poetry rooted in emotional truth. This chapbook is also valuable for writers interested in how personal narrative can be transformed into shared human experience without losing its raw edge. Offenbacher-Ferris's work is a heartfelt exploration of the human experience, inviting readers to reflect on their own journeys of love and healing.

—Munmun Samanta
Author of *Yellow Chrysanthemum*

Poet Gypsie-Ami Offenbacher-Ferris will touch your heart with tenderness at *The Arrival* of a baby girl "into the searing light painful brilliance of her existence into life."
Her *Feelings in Color* will move you through the whole spectrum of emotional light waves as she sinks into "His sea blue eyes lined with tiny rivers of broken vessels." Each one of Gypsie-Ami's poems vibrates with her own "personal catharsis" whose echoes will resonate with your own... even long after you finish reading her chapbook.

— **Christine Moughamian, M.A.**
Award-Winning Memoirist,
Organizer of The Wilmington Write To Publish Group Meetup

As she warns us in her introduction, "This is not a feel-good book." Ms. Offenbacher-Ferris' Reflections of a Woman's Life reveals a bleeding, broken heart, merciful only in its brevity.

The chapbook starts, appropriately enough, with The Arrival of a new life, still swaddled with her "mother's richest loam" where joy is tempered with the stark reality of life.

And so it is throughout this powerful collection, closing with Reflections on life and its never-ending cycle, each happiness sliced by pain, love tainted with betrayal, life with all its color ending in death.

Here you'll find raw emotions on full display, no filter, just heartfelt poems with earthy metaphors, throbbing on the page.

—Bartholomew Barker
Author of *Milkshakes and Chilidogs: And Other Food Poems*

From the moment Gypsie-Ami invites you into her written world she warns you, the reader, to be prepared for an unexpected emotional journey. And, she definitely delivers. She dives deeply into the parts of ourselves we prefer to hide away in the dark. She pulls them out into the light helping us find humor in them, how to survive them, and how to move on. Her powerful poems contain surprising insight, joy, playfulness, and at times you cry along with her.

Wordplay and lyrical rhythms provide the perfect backdrop to transport and carry the reader on a whimsical, deeply soul rooted caravan ride where writer and reader share the emotional landscape.

—Koleen K. Telecky, M.S., CCC-SLP

Gypsie-Ami Offenbacher-Ferris presents poems that are intelligent in conception and radiantly illuminating in reading. The compilation has thematic depth, presenting slices of real life. The collection is a valuable companion for poetry lovers.

—Rose-Mary Harrington, A.R.
Ammons Poetry Award 2025,
MA University of Arizona.

Reflections of a Woman's Life

A Chapbook

Gypsie-Ami Offenbacher-Ferris

This is not a feel-good book. It is not a self-help book. This is a book about love and pain. Emotional pain. Betrayal. Love lost. Love neglected. Love thrown away. New love. Love born and love reborn. It is a writing to bring about a personal catharsis and a reaching out to any and all, women, or men, who have had their hearts ripped from their body by a trusted loved one, leaving a blood-filled gaping hole that feels as though it may never heal. Let us commiserate together in the hope that we will come out the other side happy and whole, or at least intact!

Gypsie-Ami Offenbacher-Ferris

Table of Contents

The Arrival

From out of the dark abyss
she rose, scratching, clawing baby
at the solvent clogging her nose
and filling her mouth.

Ears packed with Mother's richest
loam deafening the screams of her arrival
into the searing light painful brilliance of
her existence into life.

Clutching at the foreign, warm five
fingered hands, sucking, plucking,
poking at skin rampaged by the
stinging air surrounding her.

No more that blissful sleep
that entombed darkness.
Floating, existing without air without water,
without food or the need to eat.

No sound save the distant beat
of a drum, thump thump thump thump
ever lulling her, ever coddling her
within her sanctuary.

A shrill sound alien in its pitch
and intensity assaults her ears
cleaned of debris, stabbing shards
of intermittent light attack her lidded eyes.

Finally, swaddled protectively held in gentle
swaying arms,
a presence known but unknown, presses wet,
warm lips to the newborn's face.

Chance Encounter

So delighted to see another grandmother
negotiating a stroller-filled baby.
Other shoppers appeared to be preppy
thirty-something girls
with designer prams and baby models.

Sadly, I do not fit that profile.
A touch of envy slid by,
their youth, looks and that energy all.
The other grandma drew closer,
we waved in synchronicity.

I couldn't see her well,
but I'm sure
she returned my smile.
Ecstatic babies gurgled at each other.
I moved closer and bumped into the
full-length mirror in front of me.

Embarrassed, I looked around quickly,
waved bye to myself
and fled the store.

My Garden

In my garden
my garden so serene
Calm and patience
do I toil within its dark
rich soil

Once wild with weeds
not a living flower could be seen
Colorless and windless
was its world
such toil

Beside a flower
blooming fully red
Lay a lovely dragonfly
clearly he was dead
life gone

His wings they spread
so bright and green
The sun's rays did
pass right through
shimmering on

Then just a bit further down
laying there on the ground

A tiny bird's egg
cracked open
baby bird flew away
A snake did slither
Across the grove
Rattler rattling loudly
warning me boldly
away I stayed

All at once a toad jumped up
startling me heartily
Giggling softly, I asked him
from where he came
but he didn't stay to play my game

Free

My body is an adversary
one I can not
fight
Tortured by day
tormented at night

The demon beckons
with pills to break
free
Take these lies
and follow me
Into the land of darkness
where the damned stay
interred

Come to me now
the dark spirit urged

A bright blinding light
reached from outside my
tomb
Listen not to the dark one
his way leads to doom

Suffer you will
and suffer you must
trapped
Trusting, feeling, believing
one day you'll be

Free

Nibble at the Beach

Sunset washed over us
the ray's liquid gold,
intwining our lightly browned skin
into one solid, substantial aura.

This was the one after many years,
the dating, the searching,
the broken marriage vows,
the aloneness: he was here holding me.

Divulging deep love and adoration,
heart filled with joy and pure emotion
rugged man holding me
so easily in his arms.

Brushing the hair from my eyes
ocean breeze blowing
its gentle warning.
Wind whispering into deaf ears.

Woman walking on the sand,
purposeful strides
of foreboding and purpose,
one lone woman.

Embrace dropped abruptly,
icy coldness rips
away the warmth
of his arms.

Who is that, I whisper.

My wife, he whispered in reply.

A Mother's Nose Noes

My little girl
has two little feet
as cute as they can be

On those feet
are ten little toes
pretty little digits all

Alas my little girl
grew to be a big girl
she's over six feet tall

Her pretty, little feet
now pretty, big feet
did sport ten stinky big toes

When I asked her one day
spying her shoes where they lay
Say what is that smell?

My big little girl denied
straight-faced with a whirl
she had not even a clue

But a mother's nose knows
when her little girl's toes
do stink up a room for sure

No matter how those ten toes
denied with adamant noes
it was not her foul aromatic smell

A mother does know in fact
she will always know the scent
of her little girls' ten stinky toes

There's nothing quite like it
no man-made sniffer that can rival
a mother's nose knows toes

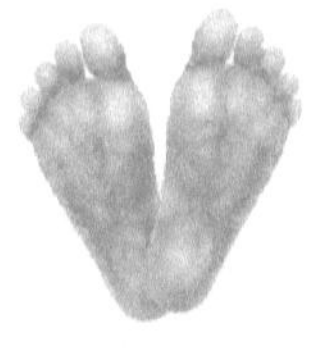

Moving On - Letting Go

carrying you myself
terrifyingly secure within me
first kick let me know you were there

many kicks more until then
your time to enter this new world
arriving just fine and exactly on time

just now I looked up to see
a young man all grown now on his
own without me not needing a mom

so, it's time to move on and let go

Feelings in Color

He entered the house,
our house surrounded by lush green bushes
heavy with welcoming pink and comforting,
yellow
flowering hibiscus.

Their scent wafting in through the white
clapboard door
he left standing open.
I could smell the richness of each flower
Bright pink sharply citrusy.

The yellow reminding me of warm, sunny days
spent on the beach as he stood there so tall, so
manly
surrounded within an aura of pastel orange
His face drawn, pinched. He knew that I knew
and he was afraid.

The orange deepened when he asked if he
could come in,
I answered in the most neutral voice I could
muster.
Much like the neutral he had insisted upon
when we chose our new carpet together.

Neutral, yes, that was how I would stay.
It's your house, no need to ask to come in,
I muttered in neutral beige.
I like beige, it's comfortable, safe.

I would stay here standing on my beige carpet
and remain neutrally beige until he responded,
that this was our house, and I felt my neutral
slip,
melting into the darker color of a green so dark
it was black.

The black became red, a red that I dare not
release,
lest it consume me then he moved towards me,
his hand imploring.
His sea blue eyes lined with tiny rivers of
broken vessels,
Had he been crying? For whom had he been
crying?

For me or for her?
Beige dissipated, fire red filled my eyes.
Filled my soul, while my once warm
beating heart, turned ice cold blue.

Reflections

To be born
Is to Live
To thrive and to grow
Is to begin

Begin to learn
To Love
Nurtured into being
To be is filled with love

Love of parents
To love one's sisters
Sweet and graceful
Tough and formidable

To fall in love
With the one for you
To love the one chosen
For a lifetime

Bearing children
To do so or not
A choice to be protected
To protect them always

To experience paralyzing grief
When parents pass away
To find a family divided by greed
Those wanting materialistic memories

Watching children grow up
To become parents themselves
While growing older and wiser
To begin life's downward journey

Body grows more feeble
To move brings on pain
Kids having grandkids
To begin the cycle over again

With Appreciation

To the wonderful people who have pushed,
prodded or cajoled me
to keep going, to keep writing.

To Viola - My purple hued soul-sister,
thank you for being you!

To Christine - Organizer, leader, supporter of
lost authors and accomplished memoirist.

To Bartholomew - Poet Extraordinaire whose
sharp-edged critiques put a finer edge
to a writer's works.

To F. E. Jones - With Love

Thank you!!

Gypsie-Ami

About the Author

Gypsie-Ami Offenbacher-Ferris lives in Southport, NC, USA. Gypsie-Ami's photographic artwork was chosen beside twenty-four other artist's works by "Up Your Arts" and the City of Southport as winners in the fourth annual pole banner art project, "Raise Up Your Arts," May through November 2026.

She is a twice published poet in Cameron Art Museum's Writers Respond to Art Program and was awarded the Certificate of Completion for completing the 2021 - 24 Hour Poetry Marathon and the 2022 - 24 Hour Poetry Marathon. Her poem "Wheels" was published in the 2021, *24 Hour Poetry Marathon Anthology*. Her poem, "The Date" has been chosen for publication in the 2022 - *24 Hour Poetry Marathon.*

She is a published author in *Whisper's & Echoes*, an on-line literary magazine and in *50 Give or Take* for her 50-word stories, "Love," "The Wedding" and "The Sleep Doctor." In

Visual Verse with her poem "Mother Earth" and several editions of *The Virtual Poetorium*. Ami is also published in *Spillwords Press* with her stories, "No Ghosts This Christmas!," "Look!" and "I Am Not A Man!"

Gypsie-Ami has had the honor of being published by *Carrot Ranch Literary Community* in their *Baby Ducks Ate My Lunch Collection* for her 99 word story, *Duckling Survival Guide*.

Gypsie-Ami writes flash fiction, short stories, creative non-fiction, and fiction as well as poetry. Her short story, "Conversations With My Neighbor" is published in the anthology, *Trouble*, by Daniel Boone Publishing. Ami received Honorable Mention in *Tales from the Moonlit Path 2021*, a yearly Halloween Issue titled *Abandoned Places Halloween Challenge*, for her short story, "Abandoned Memories." Her short story "Grandmother And The Strawberry Moon" was chosen as a semi-finalist in *Stories That Need to Be Told: The Contest*.

Gypsie-Ami's first chapbook of poetry and photography is titled *Flowers Flowers Everywhere!* She has written two stage plays to date and is currently completing her second action/adventure/romance preternatural novel.

Ami is a member of *NCWN* (North Carolina Writer's Network) and *WWN* (Women Writer's Network). Ami's core writing group and the women who literally saved her life during her COVID-19 illness, *Coastal Women's Writer's Group* of Wilmington, NC.

Ami is known to her closest friends and relatives as *Gypsie*.